INSECTS

by Bettina Bird and Joan Short

Illustrated by Deborah Savin

This edition first published in the United States in 1997 by
MONDO Publishing
By arrangement with MULTIMEDIA INTERNATIONAL (UK) LTD

The publisher would like to thank Louis N. Sorkin, BCE, Department of Entomology, American Museum of Natural History, for his assistance. The authors and publisher would also like to thank Densey Clyne, Mantis Wildlife, for her invaluable assistance in the preparation of this book.

Photograph Credits: Tony Stone Images: front cover; Phillip Green: pp. 5, 6, 8, 9 left, 12 left, 13 top right, 15 left, 16, 20, 27, 31, 41 left and bottom right, 42, 43 bottom; Adrian Horridge: p. 9 right; Densey Clyne: pp. 10, 13 left, 15 right, 37; Anthony Healy: pp. 12 right, 39, 41; Arthur Woods: pp. 13 bottom right, 26; Howard Birnstihl: pp. 43 top, 45.

Text copyright © 1988 by Bettina Bird and Joan Short
Illustrations copyright © 1988 by Multimedia International (UK) Ltd

For information contact:
MONDO Publishing
One Plaza Road
Greenvale, New York 11548

Printed in Hong Kong
First Mondo printing, January 1997
97 98 99 00 01 02   9 8 7 6 5 4 3 2 1

Originally published in Australia in 1988 by Horwitz Publications Pty Ltd
Original development by Robert Andersen & Associates and Snowball Educational
Designed by Deborah Savin   Cover redesign by Charlotte Staub

Library of Congress Cataloging-in-Publication Data
Bird, Bettina.
    Insects / by Bettina Bird and Joan Short ; illustrated by Deborah Savin.
        p.   cm. — (Mondo animals)
    "Originally published in Australia in 1988 by Horwitz Publications"— T.p. verso
    Includes index.
    Summary: Describes the physical characteristics, life cycles, and behavior of insects in general,
highlighting such types as silverfish, cicada, and butterflies.
    ISBN 1-57255-216-6 (pbk. : alk. paper)
    1. Insects—Juvenile literature. [1. Insects.] I. Short, Joan. II. Savin, Deborah, ill. III. Title. IV. Series.
QL467.2.B37   1997
595.7—dc20   96-23059
                                                              CIP
                                                              AC

Cover: Praying Mantis

CONTENTS

INTRODUCTION

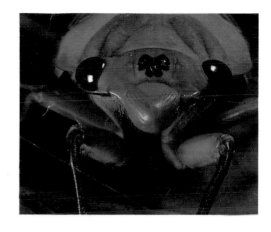

Scientists believe that there may be over a million different species of insects in the world — more than all other species of animals put together.

Butterflies, moths, beetles, cicadas, grasshoppers, dragonflies, ants, bees, flies, wasps and mosquitoes are kinds of insects, and there are many other kinds.

Left: Silk moth
Above: Cicada
Below: Wasp
Bottom: Jewel beetle

1 MAIN FEATURES COMMON TO INSECTS

Insects of all species have some features in common. Every insect has three main body parts: a head, a thorax (chest) and an abdomen. Insects of most species have six legs, but a few are legless. Adult insects of most species have two pairs of wings, but some species have only one pair and a few have no wings at all. All insects have antennae. The young of most species of insects hatch from eggs, and all young insects have enormous appetites.

The skeleton of an insect forms the outside covering of its body. This body covering is called an *exoskeleton*, which means "outside skeleton." The exoskeleton is composed of segments which fit together to cover the body and legs.

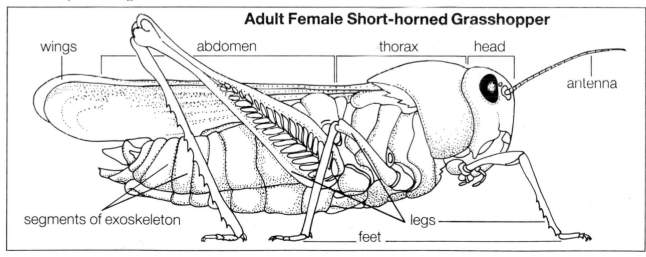

Adult Female Short-horned Grasshopper

wings   abdomen   thorax   head   antenna

segments of exoskeleton   legs   feet

Opposite: Harlequin beetles

7

The exoskeleton of an adult insect is tough, waterproof and sometimes beautifully colored. It is made mainly of a substance called *chitin*. It acts like a suit of armor to protect the insect's soft inner organs and muscles.

The exoskeleton of a young insect is, in some cases, made of a very thin layer of chitin. In other cases, it is soft like a thin skin. The young insect's exoskeleton does not stretch or grow as its muscles and inner organs increase in size. When the "skin" becomes too tight, the young insect sheds it. Underneath the old skin is a new, larger skin. Shedding an outgrown skin is called *molting*. Young insects of all species molt as they grow.

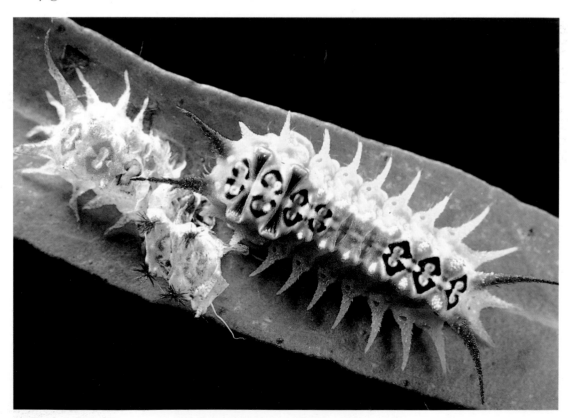

This cup moth caterpillar has shed its outgrown skin

THE BODY OF AN ADULT INSECT AND HOW IT WORKS

THE HEAD

On the head of an adult insect are the eyes, the antennae (feelers) and the mouth parts.

Eyes

Most adult insects have two large compound eyes, one on each side of the head. Each compound eye is made up of many tiny six-sided lenses that fit perfectly together. Each lens takes in a very small section of what the insect is looking at, and together these sections provide a total picture.

As well as compound eyes, many insects (such as dragonflies, grasshoppers, bees and cicadas) have three simple eyes on top of their heads. These eyes are called *ocelli*. They can distinguish only light and shade. Insects do not have eyelids so their eyes are always open.

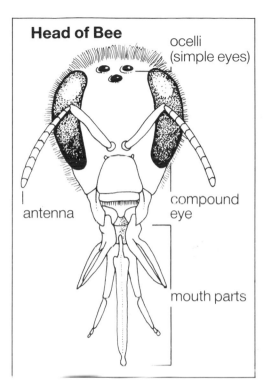

Head of Bee

ocelli (simple eyes)

antenna

compound eye

mouth parts

Far left: Compound eyes of a robber fly. The six-sided lenses fit together like the cells of a honeycomb

Left: Compound eyes and the three ocelli of a dragonfly. Each compound eye may have as many as 30,000 lenses. The ocelli form a triangle between the two compound eyes

9

Most insects must be within about three feet (one meter) of an object to see it clearly. Objects further away appear as a blur. But insects are quick to notice movement, and many can tell one color from another. The dragonfly is one of the few insects with good distance vision.

Some insects (such as the soldier and worker termites in termite colonies) are totally blind. Others have poor eyesight. These insects, as well as burrowing insects which live mostly in the dark and nocturnal insects which are active at night, rely on their senses of smell, taste and touch to find their way around.

Antennae

An insect's antennae are on the front of its head, often between the two compound eyes. The antennae are particularly sensitive to touch and smell. Some insects also use their antennae to distinguish tastes or sounds. Insects have many different types of antennae.

Above: Blind worker termites find their way around by using their highly developed senses of touch, taste and smell

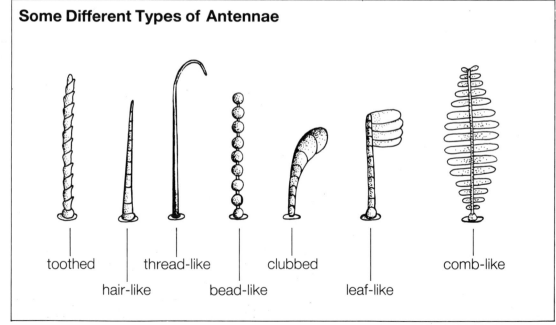

Some Different Types of Antennae

toothed
hair-like
thread-like
bead-like
clubbed
leaf-like
comb-like

10

Mouth Parts

An insect's mouth is simply a hole in the lower part of the head. A flap called a *labrum*, or lip, is attached to the top of the mouth opening. Around the mouth opening are several mouth parts which vary in shape from species to species according to the way the insect feeds.

Insects that bite and chew their food (such as grasshoppers) have two pairs of jaws. The front pair (*mandibles*) often have sharp teeth and are used for biting, tearing and chewing. The second pair (*maxillae*) are behind the mandibles. The maxillae hold the food that is in the insect's mouth and push it down the insect's throat. Both pairs of jaws move in a sideways fashion.

Insects that live on fluids like nectar and plant sap have a long tube for sucking. The sucking tube is usually called a *proboscis*. The butterfly's proboscis coils up under the insect's head when it is not feeding.

Insects that pierce plants to suck sap (such as cicadas), or the skin of animals or humans to suck blood (such as mosquitoes), have sharp, needle-like spikes called *stylets* as part of the sucking tube. The stylets help to pierce the food source.

THE THORAX

The thorax is the part of an insect's body between the head and the abdomen. An insect's legs and wings are joined to segments of the thorax. Muscles that control the movements of the legs and wings are attached to the inner walls of these segments.

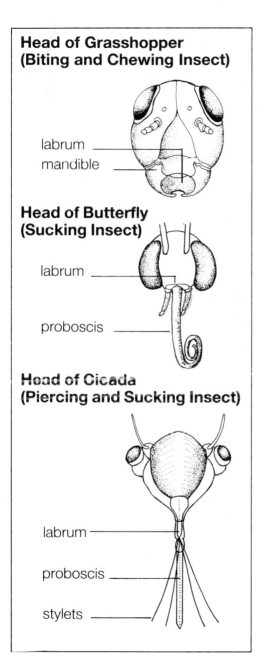

Head of Grasshopper (Biting and Chewing Insect)

labrum
mandible

Head of Butterfly (Sucking Insect)

labrum

proboscis

Head of Cicada (Piercing and Sucking Insect)

labrum

proboscis

stylets

Hind Leg of Worker Honeybee

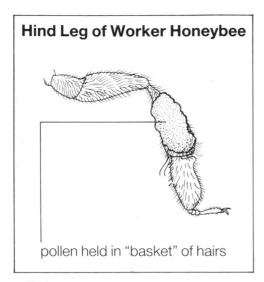

pollen held in "basket" of hairs

Above: A worker honeybee returns to the hive, its legs laden with pollen
Right: A backswimmer swims upside down through the water using hair-fringed hind legs like oars

Legs and Feet

All insects (except those that are legless) have three pairs of jointed legs. Each pair of legs is attached to a segment of the thorax. Insects' feet often have sharp claws for clinging to leaves and twigs.

Many kinds of insects have legs and feet adapted for special functions.

The hind legs of grasshoppers are long and strong so that the insects can jump quickly and cover distances many times their own length.

Some water-dwelling insects have flattened hind legs fringed with hairs which spread out when the insects are swimming. These hind legs work like oars.

The hind legs of worker honeybees have cavities for carrying balls of pollen. Long hairs on the legs make a kind of "basket" to hold the balls of pollen tightly.

Some flies have feet with sticky pads which enable them to walk upside down on the under surface of branches, leaves and petals.

The feet of butterflies have special taste sensors which help the insects to find food.

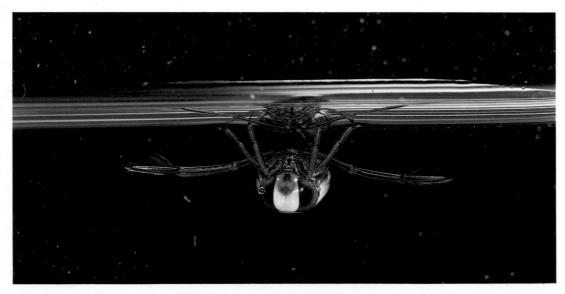

Wings

Most adult insects have two pairs of wings but some have only one pair. Each pair of wings is joined to a segment of the insect's thorax. Some insects (such as silverfish) have no wings at all.

Left: Like all butterflies the orchard butterfly has two pairs of wings

Below: Flies have only one pair of wings

Bottom: Silverfish have no wings at all

THE ABDOMEN

In the abdomen of an adult insect are the heart, the organs for digesting food and getting rid of body waste, and the reproductive organs.

The heart pumps blood to all parts of the insect's body. Insects' blood is not red like human blood, but greenish, yellowish or colorless.

The stomach and intestine digest the food that the insect eats. Waste is passed out of the anus at the rear of the abdomen.

Most female insects lay eggs. The eggs form in the ovaries then pass down the oviduct to a tube called the *ovipositor*. In many species the ovipositor extends from the rear of the female's abdomen during egg-laying.

BREATHING

An adult insect takes in oxygen from the air through tiny holes in the segments on each side of its thorax and abdomen. These holes are called *spiracles*. The spiracles lead to tubes called *tracheae* inside the insect's body. Each *trachea* leads to the system of fine air tubes, called *tracheoles*, that carries oxygen to all parts of the body. The tracheoles also carry away the waste gas, carbon dioxide.

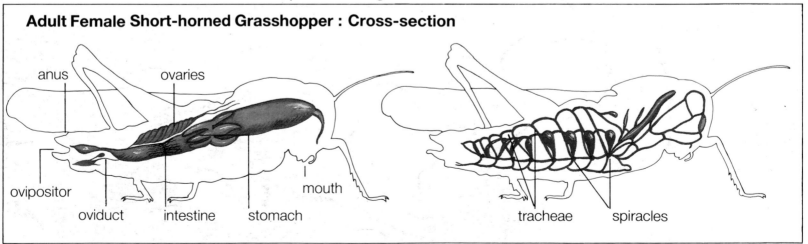

Adult Female Short-horned Grasshopper : Cross-section

anus — ovaries — ovipositor — oviduct — intestine — stomach — mouth — tracheae — spiracles

MAKING SOUNDS

No insect has a voice but many insects make sounds in other ways. It is usually the males which make sounds to attract the females. Most females are not able to make sounds, only to hear them.

Some insects make sounds by rubbing one part of the body against another. This method of making sounds is called *stridulating*. Grasshoppers stridulate by rubbing a hindleg against part of a wing.

The male cicada has a cavity in each side of its abdomen. Over each cavity is a cover which can be opened and closed. Inside is a tightly-stretched membrane, called the "drum" or *tympanum*, which can be vibrated by muscles inside the abdomen. When the cicada is "drumming," the cover opens, the membrane vibrates and the cavity acts as a sound chamber to produce a loud, throbbing, high-pitched sound.

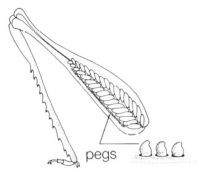

Inside Hind Leg of Male Grasshopper

pegs

A row of hard pegs on the inside leg rubs against a vein in the folded forewing to produce the grasshopper's sound

Above: Tympana on the underside of a male cicada. The cover over each tympanum is closed

Right: Long-horned grasshopper stridulating

Foreleg of Cricket, Showing Tympanal Organ

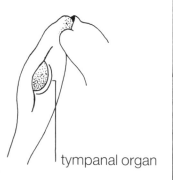

tympanal organ

Abdomen of Grasshopper, Showing Tympanal Organ

tympanal organ

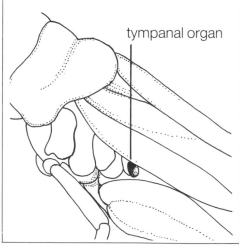

Right: The tympanal organ of this short-horned grasshopper is just visible on the side of the abdomen above the hind leg

HEARING

Most insects with well-developed sound-producing organs also have well-developed hearing organs. The hearing organs (ears) of birds and mammals are on the head but the hearing organs of insects are on other parts of the body.

Some insects have hearing organs called *tympanal organs*. Tympanal organs have thin, flat membranes which vibrate when sound waves hit them. Nerves pass messages to the insect's brain which enable it to "hear" the sound.

The tympanal organs of the grasshopper are on each side of the insect's abdomen. The cricket has tympanal organs on its front legs. The cicada has a pair of tympanal organs on the underside of the abdomen. The male cicada's tympanal membranes are in its sound-producing cavities, behind the vibrating membranes. When the male cicada is drumming, the tympanal membranes fold back so that the insect is not "deafened" by its own sound.

Other insects hear by means of delicate hairs on their antennae or on other parts of their bodies. Sound waves in the air cause the hairs to bend or vibrate and nerves send messages to the insect's brain.

2 THE LIFE HISTORIES OF INSECTS

The young of most species of insects go through various stages in development from the time they come out of the egg until they become adult insects. The development of an insect from egg to adult is generally referred to as its *life history*. In the case of most species, each stage in development results in some change of form (shape). The scientific term for "change of form" is *metamorphosis*.

Insects are divided into three groups according to how much they change in form throughout their life histories:

Group 1   Insects which undergo no change, except in size ("no metamorphosis" group)

Group 2   Insects which undergo partial change ("partial metamorphosis" group)

Group 3   Insects which undergo complete change ("complete metamorphosis" group)

GROUP 1   INSECTS WHICH UNDERGO NO CHANGE

Insects in the "no change" group emerge from their eggs looking like tiny copies of their parents. The young insects do not change noticeably in shape or color as they grow older. They change only in size. As the young grow too big for their skins they molt. Species in this group do not have wings.

Silverfish are examples of insects in the "no change" group.

SILVERFISH

Some species of silverfish are house dwellers and other species live outdoors. The body of a silverfish is covered with tiny scales which give the insect its silvery appearance and slippery feel.

After mating, female silverfish deposit their tiny eggs in cracks in woodwork if they are house dwellers, or among decaying vegetation on the ground if they live outdoors.

Like the young of all insects in the "no change" group, young silverfish look just like tiny adults when they hatch. As they grow they molt.

Young silverfish become adults when their reproductive organs are fully formed and they can begin to mate and lay eggs. Unlike other adult insects, adult silverfish continue to grow and molt until they die.

Life History of the Silverfish

(9 times life size)

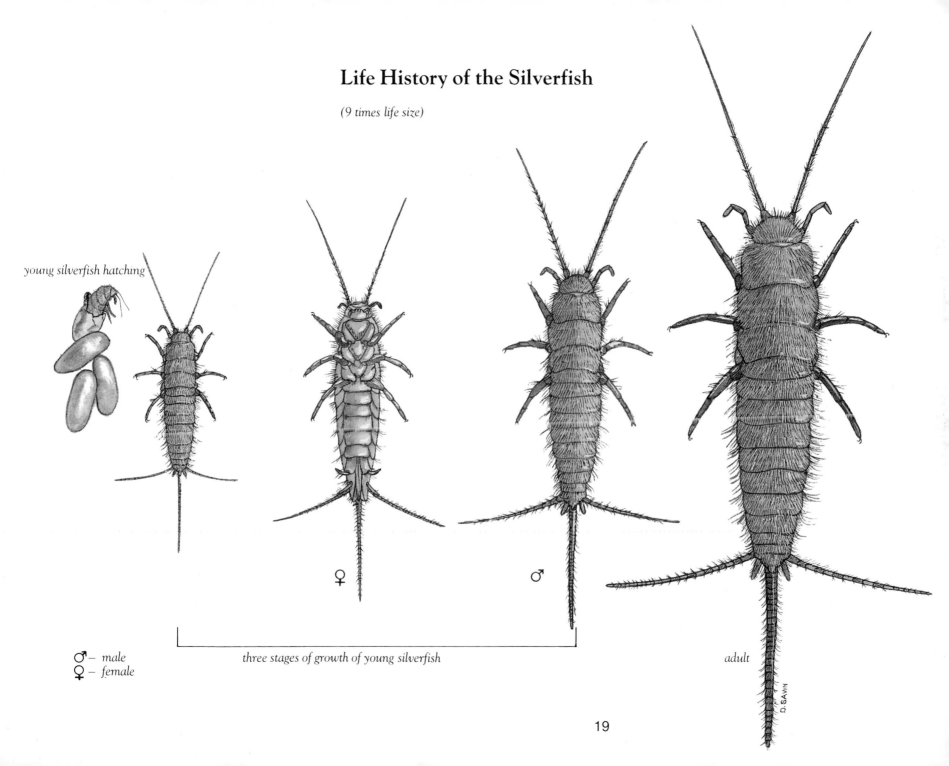

young silverfish hatching

♂ – male
♀ – female

♀

♂

three stages of growth of young silverfish

adult

D. SAVIN

GROUP 2 INSECTS WHICH UNDERGO PARTIAL CHANGE

Insects in the "partial change" group go through three main stages in development: egg, young insect (called a *nymph*), adult. Some examples of insects in this group are grasshoppers, dragonflies and cicadas.

Most adult insects in the "partial change" group have wings.

Nymphs of all insects in the "partial change" group go through changes in size, body proportion, and sometimes changes in color, from the time they emerge from the egg until they become adults. These changes take place with each molt.

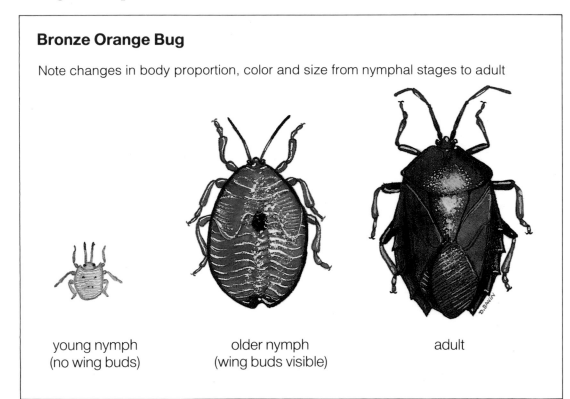

Bronze Orange Bug

Note changes in body proportion, color and size from nymphal stages to adult

| young nymph (no wing buds) | older nymph (wing buds visible) | adult |

When a nymph emerges from the egg it does not have wings, but after several molts wing buds appear. With each molt the wing buds are larger, but a nymph is never able to fly. Full-sized wings develop just before the nymph molts for the last time. When the final molt takes place, a fully winged adult emerges from the nymphal skin.

The nymphs of most kinds of insects in the "partial change" group look similar to their parents when they emerge from the eggs except that they are tiny and do not have wings. Grasshoppers are examples of typical insects in the "partial change" group.

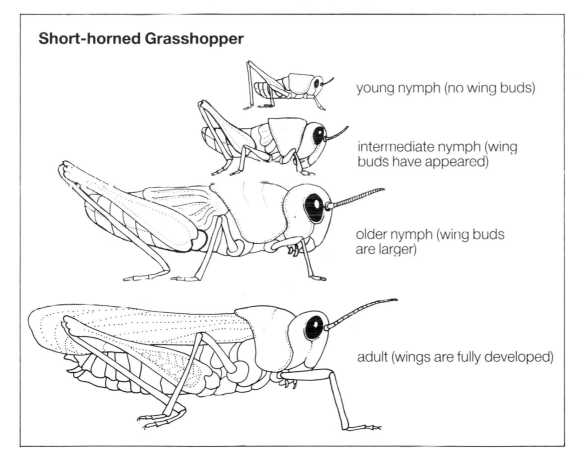

Short-horned Grasshopper

young nymph (no wing buds)

intermediate nymph (wing buds have appeared)

older nymph (wing buds are larger)

adult (wings are fully developed)

SHORT-HORNED GRASSHOPPER

Short-horned grasshoppers are often called locusts. They live and breed in most parts of the world during the warm months of the year. The stages in development of the short-horned grasshopper nymph from hatching to adulthood are similar to those of most species in the "partial change" group.

The Egg

Soon after mating, the female short-horned grasshopper prepares to lay her eggs. She uses her strong ovipositor to make a hole in the soil. As she works, her abdomen extends so that the hole is made as deep as possible. The female deposits her eggs at the bottom of the hole, then sprays a sticky substance over them to hold them together. This substance hardens into a waterproof covering called a *pod* which keeps the eggs dry. Once the eggs are laid the female grasshopper covers the opening of the hole with soil to protect the eggs from predators.

The Nymph

When the tiny grasshopper nymphs hatch they work together to force open one end of the pod. Then they work their way to the surface of the soil and hop away to begin feeding. Like their parents, grasshopper nymphs eat grass and other vegetation.

A newly hatched grasshopper nymph looks just like a tiny copy of the adult except that it does not have wings. Small wing buds appear after the second molt and become larger with each subsequent molt. The nymph molts five or six times before it is fully grown.

The Adult

When it is fully grown the grasshopper nymph is ready to molt for the last time. As the final nymphal skin splits and peels off, the adult grasshopper emerges with fully developed wings. At first the wings are soft and crumpled, but as blood pumps through their veins they expand and harden. The adult grasshopper is now ready to fly and mate.

Life History of the Short-horned Grasshopper

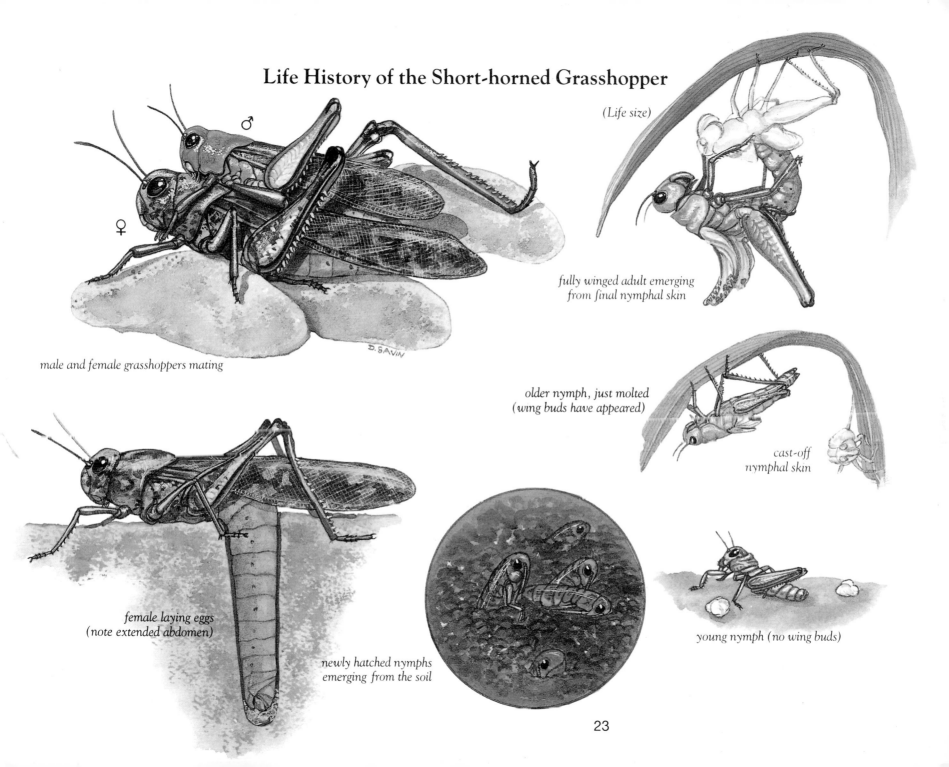

male and female grasshoppers mating

(Life size)

fully winged adult emerging from final nymphal skin

older nymph, just molted (wing buds have appeared)

cast-off nymphal skin

female laying eggs (note extended abdomen)

newly hatched nymphs emerging from the soil

young nymph (no wing buds)

23

The nymphs of more unusual kinds of insects in the "partial change" group do not look at all like their parents. In the case of these insects great changes take place inside the nymph's body before its final molt. The adult insect that emerges from the last nymphal skin looks quite different from the nymph and lives a completely different life. Dragonflies and cicadas are examples of unusual insects in the "partial change" group.

DRAGONFLY

Dragonflies are found in most parts of the world. They live near freshwater ponds, lakes and streams.

The Egg

Dragonflies mate in the warm months of the year. The method of egg-laying varies from species to species. In most cases the female dragonfly settles low down on a plant growing in water and deposits her oval eggs on the stem below water level. In other cases the female dragonfly uses her ovipositor to make slits in the stem above water level and deposits her eggs in these slits. The females of some species fly over the water and drop their eggs directly into it. The eggs sink into the mud or sand at the bottom.

The Nymph

After five to fifteen days the eggs hatch. The nymphs that hatch from the eggs laid on plant stems crawl down the stems to the bottom of the water and begin to feed. The nymphs that hatch in the mud or sand at the bottom immediately begin their search for food. Dragonfly nymphs extend a special mouth part, called a *mask*, to catch their prey. They eat tiny fish, tadpoles, mosquito larvae and the nymphs of other insects. They molt as they grow.

Dragonfly nymphs breathe through gills which take in oxygen from the water. Because they live in water, dragonfly nymphs are often called *naiads*. The word *naiad* means "water nymph."

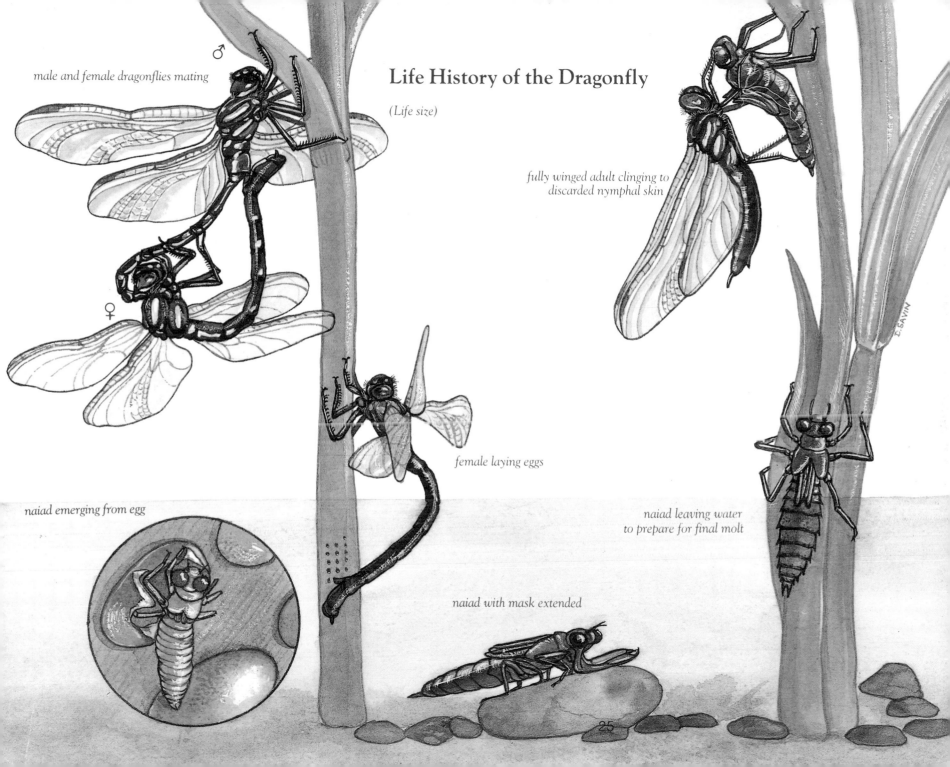

male and female dragonflies mating

♂

♀

Life History of the Dragonfly

(Life size)

fully winged adult clinging to
discarded nymphal skin

E. SAVIN

female laying eggs

naiad emerging from egg

naiad leaving water
to prepare for final molt

naiad with mask extended

25

It may take from one to five years for a dragonfly naiad to grow to full size. Then it stops feeding and settles quietly in one place while changes that have been slowly happening inside its body are completed. At last, during the night when there are few predators around, the naiad climbs up a stem into the air. It is now ready for its final molt.

The Adult

After it has left the water, the naiad rests, clinging to the stem for some hours. Then its skin splits along the back and the adult dragonfly struggles out. It turns and clings to its old, cast-off skin.

At first the dragonfly is pale and helpless and its wings are soft and crumpled. Blood pumps through the veins in its wings and they gradually expand and harden. The insect's abdomen lengthens and its soft, pale body hardens and colors.

By the time the morning sun has warmed the air the dragonfly's wings are quite firm. The adult dragonfly is now ready to fly, to feed and to mate.

Right: Cast-off skins of dragonfly naiads

Opposite: A newly emerged dragonfly clings to its discarded nymphal skin while its wings expand and its body lengthens, hardens and colors

CICADA

Cicadas live in almost all parts of the world. The high-pitched, throbbing sounds made by the males to attract females are often heard during summer.

The Egg

After mating, the female cicada lays her rows of eggs in bushes or high in trees. She makes slits in the twigs or branches with her strong, sharp ovipositor and deposits the eggs in these slits. It takes about six weeks for the eggs to hatch.

The Nymph

When they hatch, the tiny cicada nymphs are not much larger than a pin head. They drop to the ground and burrow into the soil. The nymphs feed by piercing the roots of trees with their proboscises to suck the sap. Cicada nymphs often live in the soil for several years, molting as they grow. The nymphs of some species of cicada in North America live in the soil for thirteen to seventeen years before emerging.

By the time a nymph is fully grown, important changes have taken place inside its body. The wings of the adult, and legs made for clinging rather than burrowing, have formed beneath its nymphal skin. The nymph is now ready to molt for the last time. It burrows its way out of the soil and climbs into a bush or tree. This usually happens in the late evening.

The Adult

Soon after the cicada nymph has taken up its position in the bush or tree its nymphal skin splits along the back and the adult cicada struggles free. Blood pumps through the veins in its soft crumpled wings, forcing them to spread. Once the wings have hardened, the cicada can fly away to begin its life as an adult.

Life History of the Cicada

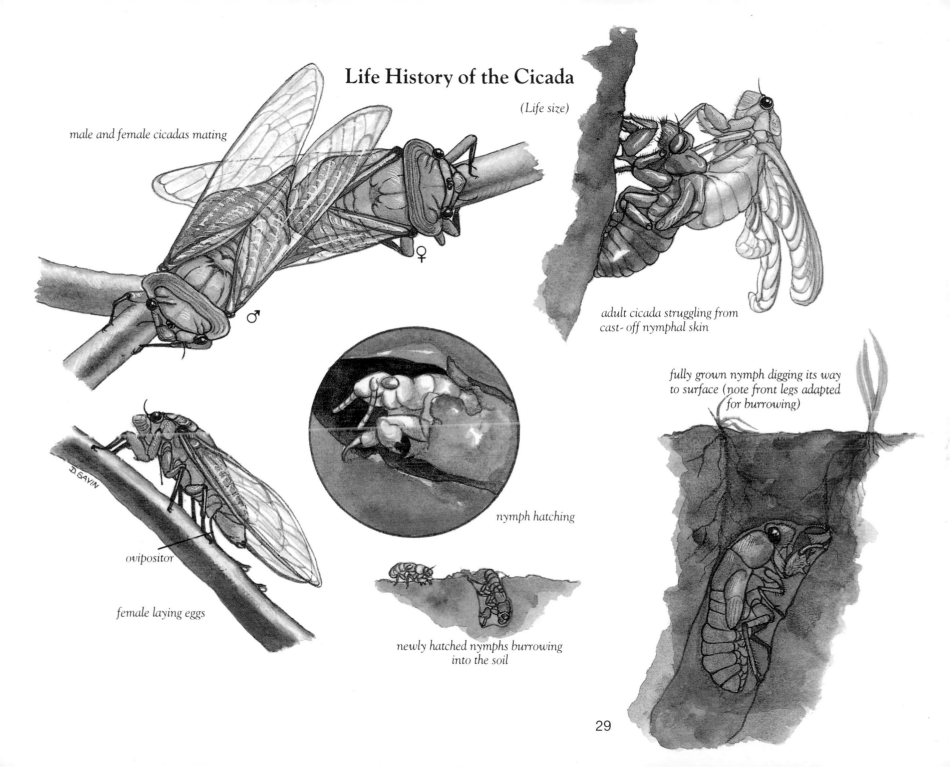

(Life size)

male and female cicadas mating

♀

♂

adult cicada struggling from cast-off nymphal skin

fully grown nymph digging its way to surface (note front legs adapted for burrowing)

D. SAVIN

ovipositor

female laying eggs

nymph hatching

newly hatched nymphs burrowing into the soil

GROUP 3   INSECTS WHICH UNDERGO COMPLETE CHANGE

Many kinds of insects go through four main stages in development during their life history: egg, larva, pupa, adult. This four-stage development is known as *complete metamorphosis*. Two examples of insects which undergo "complete change" during their life histories are butterflies and beetles.

The young of insects in the "complete change" group do not look at all like their parents at any stage of their development. The young that hatch from the eggs of these insects are called *larvae*. Many types of larvae have been given common names. The larvae of butterflies are called *caterpillars*. Beetle larvae which live under the soil or in the trunks and branches of trees are usually called *grubs*.

The larvae of all insects in the "complete change" group eventually form into *pupae*. Each species has its own special kind of pupa. When the insect is in its *pupal* stage extraordinary changes occur inside its body. When at last the pupa splits open a fully grown adult insect emerges.

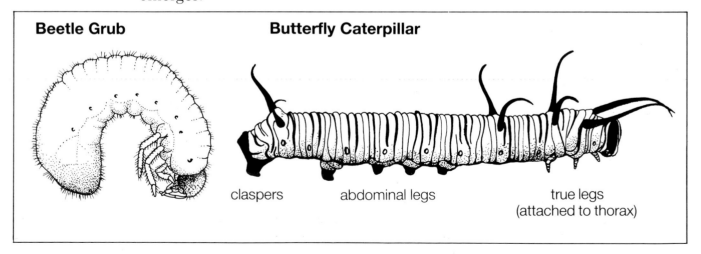

Beetle Grub   **Butterfly Caterpillar**

claspers   abdominal legs   true legs
(attached to thorax)

MONARCH BUTTERFLY

Each year, tens of millions of monarch butterflies migrate across North America. Traveling with average speeds of up to eighty miles (130 kilometers) per day, the monarch has made its way to many parts of the world. In Australia, this butterfly is called the wanderer butterfly.

The Egg

After mating, the female monarch lays her eggs on the underside of leaves of the milkweed plant. Milkweeds are the only plants on which monarch caterpillars feed. Beneath the leaves the eggs have some protection from the weather and predators.

The Larva

After a couple of weeks the eggs hatch. Like all other caterpillars, the monarch caterpillar has strong jaws for chewing leaves, stems and flowers. It also has an enormous appetite because it must store fat and other substances in its body to nourish it when it becomes a pupa.

As it grows and its skin becomes too tight the caterpillar molts.

When the caterpillar is almost fully grown, extraordinary changes begin to happen inside it. The head, eyes, sucking mouth parts and wings of the butterfly begin to form *inside* the caterpillar's body.

When the caterpillar is fully grown it stops eating and spins a little pad of silk on a stem. The strands of silk come from a spinneret on its lower lip. The caterpillar fastens its hind prolegs (claspers) to the silk pad and hangs, head down, in the air. Soon afterwards the caterpillar molts for the last time.

The Pupa (Chrysalis)

During the final molt the caterpillar's skin splits and peels off. The new skin underneath is very different from the skin it has just shed. It is called the *pupal* skin. The pupal skin is green with gold spots. The developing pupa turns and jerks for some time while it changes shape. Then the pupal skin hardens.

Inside the pupal skin some of the body parts of the caterpillar are broken down and re-formed into the body parts of the butterfly. As the butterfly develops, its legs, wings and head are pressed so hard against the inside wall of the pupal shell that their outlines can be seen from the outside. The pupa (chrysalis) stays quite still. It cannot feed or move.

The Adult

When the butterfly is fully developed the pupal shell splits open and a soft butterfly with crumpled wings struggles out. The butterfly clings to its empty pupal shell while it curls and uncurls its proboscis. Blood pumps through the veins in its wings and expands them.

When the butterfly's body covering has hardened and its wings are firm, it passes all waste fluids out of its body. The adult butterfly is now ready to fly, to feed and to mate.

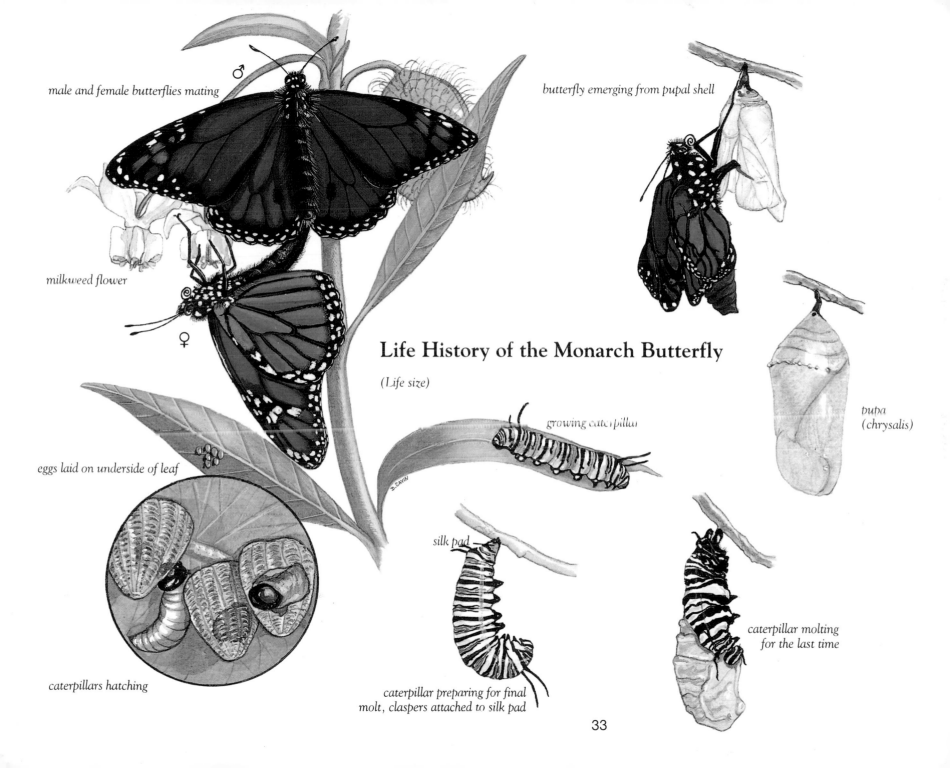

male and female butterflies mating

♂

milkweed flower

♀

butterfly emerging from pupal shell

Life History of the Monarch Butterfly

(Life size)

growing caterpillar

pupa
(chrysalis)

eggs laid on underside of leaf

B. GAVIN

silk pad

caterpillar molting
for the last time

caterpillars hatching

caterpillar preparing for final
molt, claspers attached to silk pad

33

CHRISTMAS BEETLE

The Christmas beetle is a brilliantly colored scarab beetle found in Australia. It is called the Christmas beetle because the newly developed adults emerge from their pupal cells in the soil close to Christmas, which is early summer in Australia.

Like all beetles, the Christmas beetle has a hard, shiny exoskeleton and two pairs of wings which are very different from each other. The beetle's gauzy hind wings are used for flying. The front wings, called *wing covers*, are hard and shiny like the exoskeleton and are used to protect the delicate hind wings when the beetle is not in flight. The closed wing covers give the beetle a very compact and armored appearance.

The Egg
After mating, the female Christmas beetle lays her tiny eggs on the surface of the soil.

The Larva
When the grubs hatch they burrow underground and begin their search for food. Christmas beetle larvae have strong jaws to chew the roots of plants. It takes many months for the larvae to grow to full size. They molt as they grow.

The Pupa
When a larva is fully grown it makes a small cell in the soil. It presses the soil that forms the walls of its cell very firmly. Then it becomes a pupa (*pupates*) inside this cell.

The Adult
When the adult beetle has completely formed inside its pupal shell the shell splits open and the adult beetle emerges and burrows its way to the surface of the soil. Soon it spreads its wings and flies away to feed and to mate.

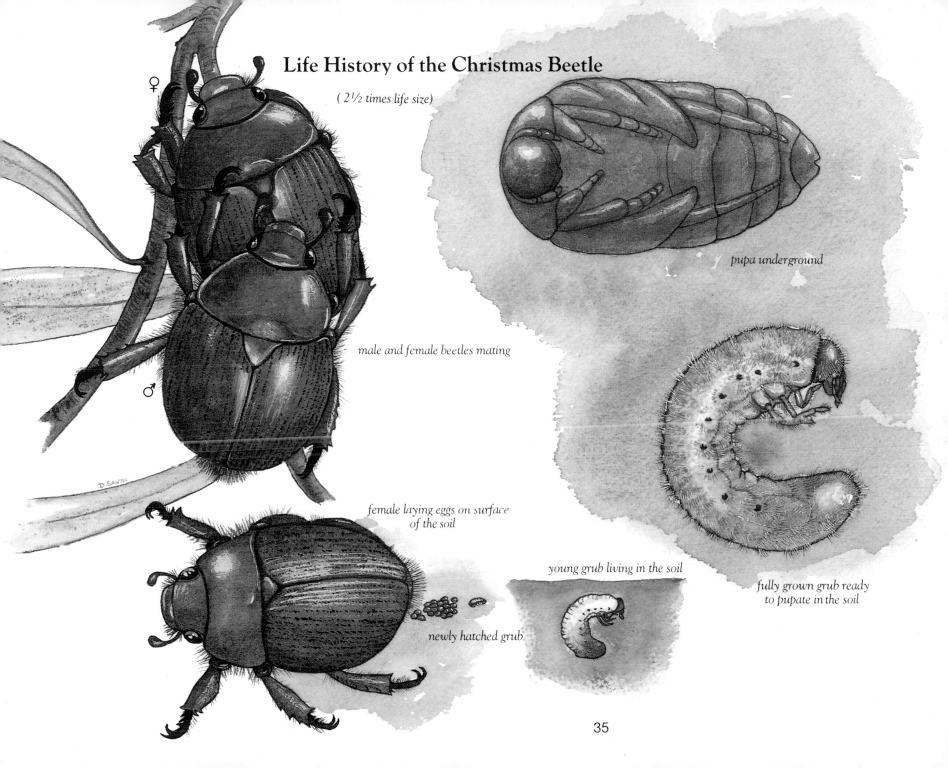

Life History of the Christmas Beetle

(2½ times life size)

♀

♂

pupa underground

male and female beetles mating

female laying eggs on surface
of the soil

young grub living in the soil

fully grown grub ready
to pupate in the soil

newly hatched grub

D.SAVIN

35

3   INSECT BEHAVIOR

All insects have patterns of behavior which help them survive. Their knowledge of what to eat, how to make sounds and how to protect themselves is inherited from their parents and built into every insect's nervous system. Because these behavior patterns are built-in, insects respond automatically to happenings in their surroundings at every stage of their development.

CATCHING PREY

Many insects are *carnivorous*. This means that they catch and eat other living creatures.

TIGER BEETLE LARVA

The tiger beetle larva is a ferocious predator. The larva waits for prey in its burrow and its sharp, curved jaws quickly grab any small creature that comes within reach. A pair of sharp hooks low down on the grub's back anchor it to the soil so that strong prey cannot drag it from its burrow.

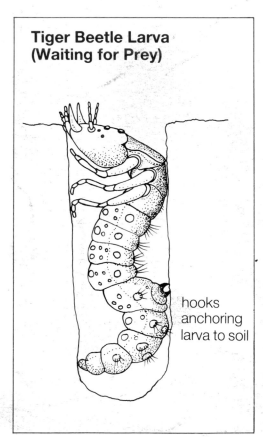

Tiger Beetle Larva (Waiting for Prey)

hooks anchoring larva to soil

PRAYING MANTIS

The praying mantis moves its head freely to watch for prey. When an insect strays close, the mantis's two front legs lash out with lightning speed to grab the victim. Rows of sharp spikes on the underside of its legs hold the victim firmly. The mantis eats its prey alive, piece by piece.

Praying mantis poised, ready to strike (note sharp spikes on front legs)

DRAGONFLY NAIAD

The dragonfly naiad's mask is an unusual device for catching prey. This special extra mouth part is like a folding arm with a pair of claw-like pincers at the end. As soon as something edible (such as a tiny fish or mosquito larva) comes within reach, the mask shoots out to catch the victim in its pincers. Then the mask brings the food back to the naiad's strong true jaws. When the mask is not in use it is folded under the naiad's head.

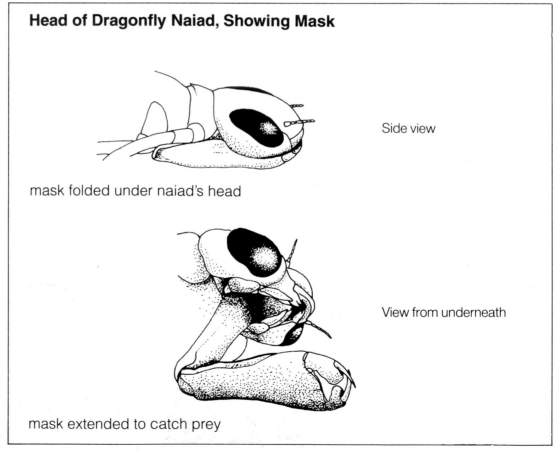

Head of Dragonfly Naiad, Showing Mask

Side view

mask folded under naiad's head

View from underneath

mask extended to catch prey

Opposite: Dragonfly naiad underwater on a plant stem. The mask is folded under the naiad's head

TRICKING PREDATORS

CAMOUFLAGE

Many insects are colored or shaped so that they blend in with their surroundings. This type of disguise is called camouflage. Camouflage helps many insects survive because it makes them difficult for their predators to detect.

Some species of moths have wing patterns like the bark of the trees on which they rest.

Stick insects can easily be mistaken for the twigs and leaves of bushes in which they live.

Some species of lacewing larvae live in aphid colonies and feed on aphids. They use an unusual method of camouflage to evade their predators. The lacewing larva's back is covered in bristles. When it has sucked out the body juices of an aphid, the larva attaches the aphid's empty skin to its own bristly back. Once it has collected a number of empty skins on its back it becomes less visible to its predators.

The larva of a case-bearing moth spins a silk "case" or "bag" in which it lives. As it spins, it attaches twigs, bark, moss or leaves to the outside as camouflage.

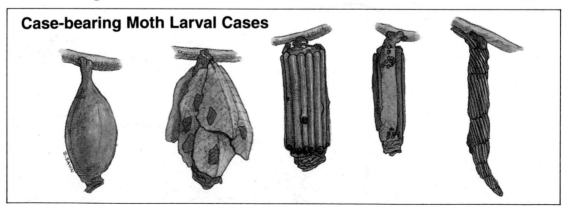

Case-bearing Moth Larval Cases

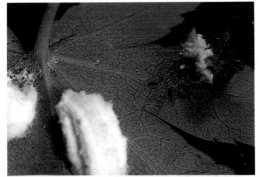

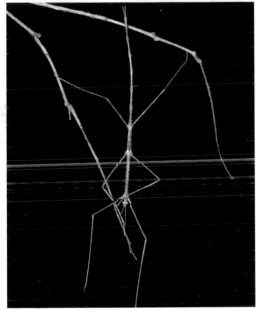

Left: This moth is almost invisible on the bark on which it rests

Above: A stick insect blends with the twigs on which it waits for prey

Top: This species of lacewing larva attaches wax from scale insects, rather than empty aphid skins, to its bristly back as camouflage

WARNING COLORATION

The bright color patterns of many insects are a warning to predators to keep away. Brightly-colored insects may have poisonous stings or be able to squirt poisonous chemicals at predators.

When a keen-sighted predator (such as a bird or mammal) attempts to eat one of these brightly-colored insects it may be stung. It soon learns to recognize the warning coloration and leaves this species of insect alone.

The yellow and black stripes of some wasps are an example of warning coloration. These wasps have a very painful sting.

The bright coloring of the ladybug is a warning that it is not good to eat. When a ladybug is attacked it secretes a nasty-tasting fluid from its leg joints.

Many kinds of cup moth caterpillars use warning coloration as well as stinging hairs to protect themselves from predators. When a predator touches the caterpillar, its stinging hairs extend to ward off the attacker.

The warning coloration and stinging hairs of a cup moth caterpillar

Top: The bright coloring of a ladybug warns predators that it is not good to eat

Left: This brightly-colored wasp has a painful sting

4 INSECTS AS SURVIVORS

Insects are the most successful creatures on Earth at survival. One reason for this is that most insects are so small. They can live in spaces that are too small for other creatures. Leaf-miners, for example, live between the thin walls of leaves.

Another reason for the survival of insects is that most adult insects have wings. This enables them to escape their predators and to fly long distances to find food and mates. Most insects lay so many eggs that some of the young are sure to survive to adulthood to breed.

However, perhaps the main reason that insects are so successful in their struggle to survive is that they can adapt to living in such a wide variety of habitats. Insects are found almost everywhere on Earth — in icy waste lands, in scorching hot deserts, in forests, on grassy plains, on the tops of high mountains, in deep caves, in freshwater rivers and lakes, in gardens and houses, and even on the surfaces of the oceans. The only place where insects cannot survive is underwater in the great salty seas and oceans of the world.

The dragonfly flies long distances to feed and to mate

LIFE HISTORY CHART

The following chart lists the kinds of insects that belong in each life history group.

1 "NO CHANGE" GROUP	2 "PARTIAL CHANGE" GROUP	3 "COMPLETE CHANGE" GROUP
silverfish springtails	bugs (includes backswimmers) cicadas cockroaches crickets dragonflies earwigs grasshoppers leaf hoppers lice mantises mayflies stick insects stoneflies termites	ants bees beetles butterflies fleas flies lacewings mosquitoes moths wasps

PRONUNCIATION GUIDE

chitin (*kite*-in)
chrysalis (*kris*-a-lis)
labrum (*lay*-brum)
larvae (*lar*-vee)
maxillae (mak-*sil*-ee)
metamorphosis (met-a-*mor*-fo-sis)
naiad (*nay*-ad)
nymph (nimf)
ocelli (oh-*sell*-eye)
ovipositor (oh-veh-*poz*-i-ter)
proboscis (pro-*bos*-is)
pupa (*pu*-pa)
pupae (*pu*-pee)
trachea (*tray*-kee-a)
tracheae (*tray*-kee-ee)
tracheoles (*tray*-kee-ols)
tympanal (*tim*-pa-nal)
tympanum (*tim*-pa-num)

INDEX

Note: Page numbers in italic refer to information provided only in photographs, illustrations or captions.